The Inspirational Story of Baseball Superstar David Ortiz

Copyright 2015 by Bill Redban - All rights reserved.

This document is geared towards providing exact and reliable information in regards to the topic and issue covered. The publication is sold with the idea that the publisher is not required to render accounting, officially permitted, or otherwise, qualified services. If advice is necessary, legal or professional, a practiced individual in the profession should be ordered.

In no way is it legal to reproduce, duplicate, or transmit any part of this document in either electronic means or in printed format. Recording of this publication is strictly prohibited and any storage of this document is not allowed unless with written permission from the publisher. All rights reserved.

The information provided herein is stated to be truthful and consistent, in that any liability, in terms of inattention or otherwise, by any usage or abuse of any policies, processes, or directions contained within is the solitary and utter responsibility of the recipient reader. Under no circumstances will any legal responsibility or blame be held against the publisher for any reparation, damages, or monetary loss due to the information herein, either directly or indirectly.

The information herein is offered for informational purposes solely, and is universal as so. The presentation of the information is without contract or any type of guarantee assurance.

The trademarks that are used are without any consent, and the publication of the trademark is without permission or backing by the trademark owner. All trademarks and brands within this book are for clarifying purposes only and are the owned by the owners themselves, not affiliated with this document.

Table Of Contents

Introduction

Chapter 1: Early Childhood & Family Life

Chapter 2: Youth

Chapter 3: Professional Life

Chapter 4: Personal Adult Life

Chapter 5: Philanthropic/Charitable Acts

Chapter 6: Legacy, Potential & Inspiration

Chapter 7: Notable Statistics & Career Milestones

Conclusion

Introduction

As the title already implies, this is a short book about [The Inspirational Story of Baseball Superstar David Ortiz] and how he rose from his life in the Dominican Republic to becoming one of today's leading and most-respected baseball players. In his rise to superstardom, David has inspired not only the youth, but fans of all ages, throughout the world.

This book portrays the key moments that David has had to go through during his early childhood years, his teen years, and up until he became what he is today. A notable source of inspiration is David's service to the community and his strong connection with the fans of the sport. He continues to serve as the humble, hard-working superstar in a sport that needs positive role models.

Combining incredible strength, patience at the plate, high baseball IQ, and superior coordination, David has shown the ability to change the outcome of any game. From being a phenom man-child to becoming one of the greatest ball players of his generation and one of the greatest Red Sox hitters ever, you'll learn here how this man has risen to the ranks of the best baseball players today.

Thanks again for grabbing this book. Hopefully you can take some of the examples from David's story and apply them to your own life!

Chapter 1:

Early Childhood & Family Life

On November 18th, 1975 in Santo Domingo, Dominican Republic, the world welcomed David Ortiz. Despite some uncertainty regarding David's birth date during his time in the Majors, documents have authenticated his age.

Some people who have watched David as a professional, note that he has tremendous natural leadership abilities. He may have developed this from being the oldest of four children. After all, throughout his youth, David served as the calming influence of the family. He developed his sense of humor and powerful inter-personal skills during this time as well.

David held much regard for his loving father, Enrique, and mother, Angela. His father, who's common nickname was "Leo", was a successful baseball player in his own right, having been a solid player in the Dominican professional leagues. Through this positive influence, David learned the game of baseball from a very technically sound teacher.

Throughout his youth, David attended professional games in his hometown and developed idols to look up to. One of these idols was Pedro Martinez, who would later become one of David's favorite teammates with the Boston Red Sox.

David's father was not an especially powerful man and did not fall into the "slugger" category. However, David won the genetic lottery with his above-average height and intimidating build at a young age. He was the type of kid who could drive the ball farther than almost anyone his age, every time he went to play. Some of the other kids his age were in awe of his long drives, often cheering him on.

His goal was to drive in runs and swing for the fences. This slugging philosophy stuck with David throughout his entire playing career and because of that, he has always played the role of power hitter.

Chapter 2:

Youth

When David first arrived at Estudia Espallat High School, he began to excel at a second sport - basketball. Because he towered over most of his peers, his size gave him a great advantage on the court. His hand-eye coordination and power translated from baseball to basketball and he enjoyed success leading his team.

Because David filled out so quickly, there were scouts who took notice and kept him on their radar. Many predicted the young Dominican could become a power hitter who could play in the United States, at least in the Minor Leagues. However, what was the most surprising skill that

David possessed was his ability to control his swings. David was not overly aggressive if he saw a pitch that he wasn't fond of. Unlike most young players who were physically dominant, David did not buy into the hype that he could knock everything out of the park.

His knowledge of how to wait for the right pitch, as well as how to hit to the opposite field, made him wise beyond his years. He knew how to foul off pitches and stay reserved at the plate. In essence, he was confident in his ability to out-duel the pitchers he faced, no matter how nasty their pitches were.

As an added bonus, David transferred his relaxed attitude from his family life onto the baseball field. He did not get noticeably flustered if he had a bad day at the plate. Likewise, if he went 5 for 5, you wouldn't see him get too high on himself - he was the definition of even-keel.

After a successful high school career as a sports star, David graduated in 1992 from Estudia Espallat High School. The Seattle Mariners, who were very high on David's potential, jumped on the opportunity to snag him before anyone else. They drafted him in 1992 at around the same time of his high school graduation. He had just turned seventeen at the time.

Chapter 3:

Professional Life

David spent a season with the Dominican Summer League club for Seattle, he appeared in 61 games and hit .264 with a total of 35 extra-base hits. He later joined Peoria, one of Seattle's affiliate teams. At the beginning of this journey, David really had a tough time adjusting to the speed and rhythm of the Minor Leagues. He struck out almost one time per game and his batting average was just under .250. However, David did show a surprising amount of agility for his size on the defensive side of the ball. His percentage of put-outs vs. total chances was the highest in the league.

His second attempt in Peoria was in 1995. This time there were some new faces in the clubhouse, including Joe Mays and Ramon Vazquez. At the ripe age of nineteen years old, David finally provided the full productive season that Seattle scouts had hoped for. He maintained a 19-game hitting streak during the months of June and July, while ending the year with a batting average of above .330. His slugging numbers were impressive as well, with almost 20 doubles and 37 RBIs, his defensive skills were on par with the previous season, leading the league in fielding percentage once again. In recognition of his efforts, the Seattle organization named David the MVP of the club and he was selected as an All-Star for the league.

Before long, David was promoted for the 1996 season to Class-A in the Seattle organization. At only 20 years of age, David showed that he had the potential to play for the Mariners one day. He finished the season as one of the best players on the team and was recognized as an All-Star once again. Once again, he was considered one of the best defensive first basemen in the league.

After showing the Mariners that he deserved a shot at the Major Leagues, David was expecting to be called up soon. However, during the month of August, the Mariners received Dave Hollins from the Minnesota Twins in exchange for a player that would be decided later. Within a month, Minnesota and Seattle agreed to send David to the Twins as part of that deal.

David received this news while he was at home in the Dominican Republic. As you would expect by now, David took this news in stride, with an optimistic view of the future. Increasing his spirits even more, David realized that the Twins had noticeable voids at first base and DH, the two positions David was best suited for. Paul Molitor, who was their incumbent at the DH position, was going to retire in the near future, as he was already 40 years old.

At this time, David expressed his interest in going by the last name "Ortiz" rather than "Arias" as a professional player. David's request was granted and he began the 1997 season with the Fort Myers Miracle, Minnesota's Class-A affiliate. From the start, David was wowing the competition and his coaches alike. His batting average was over .400 in the first eleven games, knocking in 22 RBIs and 5 home runs. He earned Player of the Month honors for this red-hot start to the season.

Within a matter of weeks, David was promoted to the Class-AA level. Without showing any signs of an adjustment period, David continued to dominate his competition. His batting average was close to .380 after 30 games of play. After such a large sample size, it was obvious that David's scorching hot play was not a streak of luck or happenstance. Once again, David was promoted within the season.

Finally, David reached the level just beneath the Majors, Class-AAA. His statistics leveled out a bit, and David looked less like a man amongst boys in terms of numbers, but nonetheless, the Twins were already convinced. By September, David found himself in the Major Leagues, and got his first hit during his second game of play.

As you can imagine, David had an extremely long season, both mentally and physically. Not only did he jump through the rankings from the lowest level to the highest level all in one season, but he actually had the highest amount of at-bats for any player within the organization. He had an astronomical 664 total plate appearances for the duration of the season!

The Twins started the 1998 season with an open competition for the first base starting job, and David was one of the candidates competing. Unfortunately, David displeased his manager with an apparent lack of effort on the defensive side of the ball. His manager, Tom Kelly, began to personally work with David on his defense in hopes that he would be able to turn it around.

Working in David's favor was the fact that he was still sharp at the plate, including putting together a seven-game hit streak in the early part of the season. However, just as David was finding his groove, his right wrist suffered a fracture in one of the bones, which resulted in his inactivity until the end of June.

To rehabilitate and get a feeling for live ball, David played a short period with the Class-AAA affiliate, before being called back up to the Twins. Despite Minnesota not being in contention for a playoff position in the American League, David worked at creating a name for himself and showing that he belonged in the league as a full-time player. He completed the season with a solid stat line - nine home runs to go along with 46 RBIs, finishing with a batting average of .277.

David entered the following season expecting a spot as the starter, however, after a slow start in Spring Training, it was decided that David would benefit from another season of experience in the Minor Leagues. However, David did not agree with this premise and he believed that he earned his place as a regular player for the Twins. The Twins told him that he needed to improve on his defense and become more disciplined at the plate if he wanted another shot.

In response, David absolutely destroyed the Minor Leagues, ruthlessly knocking fly balls deep out of the park and driving in baserunner after baserunner. There was no way David would be denied another chance at the next level and he made sure of it. By September, he was called back up for another shot to show what he could offer. After finishing with a grand total of zero hits in his twenty at-bats, David felt embarrassed and went to work on his game during the offseason. In the Dominican Winter League, David played so hard that he finished just short of winning the league's Triple Crown award.

After seeing his dream almost slip away from him, David made sure that the following professional season would cement his status as a key player for the organization. He entered the 2000 season by hustling on defense, taking extra batting practice swings, and lost some extra weight. As a result, he earned himself time at first base as well as DH. To help David's cause, Minnesota knew that they were not going to contend for the playoffs that season after having finished at the bottom of the American League Central in the previous campaign.

The Twins roster featured mostly young talent who lacked experience. The Twins were hoping that the season could help these players mature and develop their team chemistry, in hopes to build for the future. By the end of the season, the Twins finished with less than seventy wins but showed hope for the next season and beyond. The young talent had matured as expected and some players were starting to show promise. David was included in this group, along with players such as Torii Hunter and LaTroy Hawkins. David finished the season with over one hundred hits and a .282 batting average. Most importantly, his defense was much improved, as he only committed one error all season.

In the following year, the Twins surprised most people around the league, even their own fans. Their young talent continued to improve, while Brad Radke and the starting rotation was greatly improved from the season before. Minnesota was able to create a five-game lead in the

American League Central by the All-Star break. Unfortunately, the Twins' bullpen was not able to hold up during the entirety of the pennant race, which led the Twins to fade out down the stretch. However, the team still finished with a record above .500, a great improvement from the previous season.

The Twins were in desperate need of a difference-making player to keep up during the race, and David could have become that player. However, after fracturing his wrist, David ended up on the DL and was not able to return until the end of July. Still impeded by the recovery process, David did not possess the old form of his swing, which led him to pursue pitches and his production plummeted. Luckily, he was able to work with batting coach Scott Ullger, who helped to work out the kinks in David's swing.

Just when David seemed to be getting everything back in stride, he suffered an unexpected tragedy to his family life. His mother died in an accident on New Year's Day. At this point, just like for anybody else in a similar situation, David had two options - he could either let this negatively effect his day to day life, or he could use this event as motivation to become better than ever before. David chose the latter, as he dedicated himself to his craft like never before. David's teammates rallied around him and he appreciated the love sent his way by players and fans.

After a slow start to the season and running into a few injury issues, David finally got his groove back in time for the second half of the season. He proceeded to hit at a .419 mark and knock in seven home runs to go along with 18 RBIs in the three weeks after the All-Star break. It translated into team success, as the Twins were able to grab a solid lead in the American League Central playoff race. After finishing the season on top of the division, Minnesota was back to relevance and back in the playoffs.

The Twins were able to get to the second round of the playoffs before losing to the Angels. However, they were able to show the world that they could be a serious contender going forward. David had his best season yet, knocking in 20 home runs, 32 doubles, and 75 RBIs, despite only playing in three quarters of the season.

Boston

At this point, David earned the right for arbitration, his current salary of $900,000 was ready to take a bump up to $2 million. Unfortunately, the Twins were not in position to commit to David long-term and were not convinced that he would become an All-Star caliber player. By the end of the year, the Twins released David from the roster.

One of David's close friends, Pedro Martinez, a man who David viewed as an older brother throughout his life, was currently playing for the Boston Red Sox. As a true friend would, Pedro convinced his General Manager, Theo Epstein, to give David a chance on a one-year deal worth a little over $1 million.

Despite the fact that Boston offered him a deal, David was not sure that he would get playing time on the field. While David's role on the field was not clear, his personality in the clubhouse really shined through. In the locker room, David was able to mesh with the wide variety of players on the roster. From Manny Ramirez to Pedro Martinez, David was the one who could understand each individual.

His light-hearted personality enabled him to take jokes and not get flustered as the new guy. It was publicly known that the team had a number of odd personalities and was probably the most difficult roster to manage in all of baseball. David made that job a little easier.

After some time, David showed that he could take over the role of DH as a full-time player. By the beginning of August, David became a lock in the everyday line-up. He came up big in the clutch and turned into a fan favorite because of the way he would kill the New York Yankees, the Red Sox' biggest rival. He learned to become more patient at the plate and he was able to draw more walks while striking out less, thanks in big part to Ron Jackson, his batting coach.

Despite a great year for the organization, the Red Sox came up short in the second round of the the American League playoffs. They took the

Yankees to a Game 7, but lost because of the legendary home run that Aaron Boone hit in the 12th inning. This play will be forever remembered by both the Yankees and Red Sox fan bases, but through much different sentiments. Nevertheless, David showed Red Sox management that he could perform in the biggest moments and could be the starting DH going forward.

Despite what one would consider a successful season for most clubs, Theo Epstein wanted to make a change at the top, the Sox franchise changed to Terry Francona at manager and changed their top ace to Curt Schilling. Theo also gave David a two year deal that was worth $12 million. In typical fashion, David wanted to prove his doubters wrong and take his game to the next level.

The Red Sox were playing like an average team through the beginning of the year, but David was on a tear, leading the entire American League in RBIs and doubles. He ended up making the All-Star team and enjoyed a rising surge in popularity amongst fans (many who were casual fans).

After a trade involving Nomar Garciaparra around the trade deadline, the Red Sox turned it around. By the end of the season, they almost totaled 100 wins and solidified their spot in the American League Wild Card race. They did so well that they were actually in contention to possibly win the pennant from the Yankees. However, they ran out of games and the Yankees maintained their lead.

During this season, David earned his nickname "Big Papi". The nickname was given to him by his teammates because of his physical build and loving personality. The season served as a breakout year for David, finally being recognized as one of the elite sluggers in the game. There was even talk around the league that he should be considered for the American League MVP award. In total, he hit for an average of just over .300, almost 50 doubles, over 40 home runs, and almost 140 RBIs.

The Red Sox made it past the Angels in the first round and found themselves in the same position as the year before, facing the Yankees in the second round. After struggling in the first three games, the Red Sox found themselves in a 0-3 hole. Not only did they lose the third game, but the final score was 19-8. To make matters worse, no team had ever come back from such a deficit to win a series.

But David had faced plenty of adversity up until that point in his life and he was ready for the challenge. The Red Sox were able to tie Game 4 by breaking through against Mariano Rivera. In extra innings, David saved the day with a walk-off home run, his second of the post-season. After taking their first victory of the series, the Red Sox tried to capitalize on the momentum by winning Game 5. Guess who found themselves at the plate in another walk-off situation? Big Papi was able to hit a clutch single that brought home the winning run.

As the series headed back to New York City, Curt Schilling dominated Game 6 and set the team up for the potential to make history, as the only club to come back from a 0-3 deficit.

Guess who came to play in Game 7? Big Papi, once again. In his first plate appearance, David hit a home run off of Kevin Brown, giving the Red Sox players confidence. Thanks to the help of a great pitching game by Derek Lowe, the Red Sox won by seven and advanced to the World Series. Not surprisingly, David was awarded the

ALCS MVP award as he totaled three home runs to go along with 11 RBIs.

Using the momentum they had built up, Boston dominated the St. Louis Cardinals, sweeping them convincingly. The championship marked the first for the franchise since the year 1918. The dramatic end to the season helped make "David Ortiz" a household name for even the most casual of baseball fans. He took it all in stride, showing the world that his warm personality was the right fit for the fame that he was met with.

Post-2004

David met the high standards that were set for him with another great season in 2005. He totaled 47 home runs, almost half of them being in game-tying or game-leading situations, solidifying his image as a clutch player. David knocked in almost 150 runs, leading all of MLB in RBIs. He also led the team's hitters in almost all important statistical categories. The Sox went on to lose in the first round of the playoffs.

In the 2006 season, injuries and aging took its toll on the Red Sox. They did not perform well, but David had his best year ever. He dominated seemingly every night, knocking out 54 home runs, 137 RBIs and drawing 119 walks. His plate presence was incredible, almost like other sluggers of the decade, such as Barry Bonds and Albert Pujols. He reached that level to where opposing pitchers literally feared him coming to the plate and tried to throw around him just so that they didn't risk giving up a blast to the upper deck. Despite his great individual success, the team did not make the playoffs in 2006.

In 2007, David helped lead Boston to another World Series championship. During the regular season, David totaled 35 homers and almost 120 RBIs, all while hitting for an average of .332. By the end of the year, David was fourth in voting in the AL MVP race. Most importantly for him though, he was able to come through in the World Series, completely dominating at certain times and was able to lead the offense to a sweep against the Colorado Rockies.

In 2008 and 2009, David was battling injuries and missed several weeks interspersed throughout the seasons, causing him to struggle to find a rhythm. However, he did reach some career milestones within that period. On July 9th of 2009, David was able to hit his 300th career home run against the Kansas City Royals, while playing at home in front of the Red Sox fans.

2010 marked a comeback year for David, as he knocked in over 100 RBIs and more than 30 home runs, instilling fear into the pitchers once again. To top it off, he won the Home Run Derby contest during the All-Star Game festivities, something that is definitely a plus for a person that views themselves as a slugger.

In 2011, David had another productive season, hitting almost 30 home runs and 100 RBIs, with a batting average of over .300. Most importantly for his legacy, David was awarded the Roberto Clemente Award for his charitable work off of the baseball field. For someone as loving as David is, he probably felt just as happy about his recognition for off-field efforts as he does for his on-field accomplishments.

2012 was an injury plagued year for David as he struggled with recovery in his Achilles tendon. Luckily he was able to recover with no significant impact on his playing status, especially because he was getting older in his career. In 2013, the Red Sox entered the season as a dark-horse candidate to win the World Series. However, throughout the year, they began to develop amazing chemistry and were able to stay relatively healthy. David was able to reach vintage form, as he knocked in 30 home runs and over 100 RBIs, finishing with a batting average of .309. By the end of the season, he ranked in the top 10 in the American League for all three of these categories.

Most importantly, David showed that he still had that clutch gene that seemed to always show up in big moments. For the entirety of the 2013 postseason, David totaled 13 RBIs and served up 5 homers. He dominated the World Series once again, hitting for an average of .688... yes, you read that correctly, he hit for an average of .668 in the World Series! In one of the greatest World Series performances in recent history, Big Papi showed that he still had "it" and that no moment is too big for him.

Hitting Style

If you've ever seen David standing next to normal sized human beings, you've probably noticed that he has the typical build of a slugger - massive and intimidating. However, what sets him apart from most guys who have comparable size and strength is his intelligence and mental approach to the game.

He has the ability to hit to any part of the field and will not waste swings on pitches he doesn't like. Also, he's not an easy out for left-handed pitchers like many other lefties, many who are in the pros.

He can send pitches out of the park, despite the location, and has greatly improved his ability to pull the inside fastball, up by his hands. This used to be a weakness for him when he first came into the league. To see how much he's improved, ask a pitcher today how comfortable they feel about throwing that pitch to Papi with the game on the line.

David also has the ability to change his mindset during an at-bat if he feels that the opposing pitcher is trying to use a sly technique on him or if the defense has shifted for him. He may have been young and inexperienced at one point, but he's rarely going to look foolish at this point in his career.

Chapter 4:

Personal Adult Life

In his personal life, David is known for being very likable and humble in his day to day interactions. As an example, David has made it a point that each time he hits a home run, he looks to the sky and points his pointer fingers up, as to signal a tribute to his mother, Angela. Because she only died at the age of 46, and before David hit his prime, he makes it a point to live a life that would make her proud if she were still here. Also, David sports a tattoo of his mother on his arm, specifically his bicep, as a tribute to her life.

David married his wife, Tiffany, a decade ago and they have been through a lot during their marriage. They currently have three children and she has even been able to convert David into a Green Bay Packers fan, as she is a native of Wisconsin. They contemplated divorce at one point but later decided that they would continue their relationship and were able to work through whatever troubles they had.

Even though David has been living in the United States for some time, it was not until 2008 that he became a United States citizen. He became a citizen in Boston at the John F. Kennedy Library.

Because of his powerful persona, a variety of companies have jumped at the opportunity to have him sponsor their products and services. David has worked with companies like Reebok and others in mutual deals. Reebok even created baseball cleats for David, called the "Big Papi".

As a side business venture, David opened a night club called "Forty-Forty" inside of his home country of Dominican Republic.

Chapter 5:

Philanthropic/Charitable Acts

In 2007, Big Papi created his own fund called "The David Ortiz Children's Fund". The purpose of his fund is to support the wide range of causes that David believes in. In essence, it gives David the ability to effectively donate to children who really need his support and he is able to disperse these funds in whichever locations he wants to. He has mainly focused on helping the youth in his home country of Dominican Republic and his new home of Boston, Massachusetts.

To help raise even more funds, David created a Charity Wine label that he called "Vintage Papi".

The proceeds from the sales of these labels go directly to his fund to benefit the underprivileged youth. As of today, this wine has gone on to raise over $150,000.

On April 20th, 2013, in a well publicized show of emotion, Papi told the citizens of Boston, "This is our [expletive] city, and no one is going to dictate our freedom. Stay Strong." This was in response to the Boston Marathon bombings that brought stress to many people in the town. This was significant for the fan base because it occurred only a few days after the tragedy of the bombings and it was also the first game David played at Fenway Park since his achilles injury from August of the previous year.

Unexpectedly, the people of Boston were so driven by his passion that they wanted baseball bats to be produced with his quote on them. Their demands were met and the bats were produced. The proceeds were used to help the people who were impacted by the bombings.

However, if you know anything about Boston fans, you know that they are die-hard for their sports. Thanks to the supporters, the project raised over $30 million and made a huge impact in the community. The Red Sox organization also donated to the cause. Big Papi presented the checks publicly to the Mayor of Boston as a sign of accomplishment for the city.

David has also been a big supporter of health care for children. Since the creation of his fund, David has personally gone to the Dominican Republic multiple times to donate checks to the hospitals of his choice. Through sponsorships, auctions, and using fundraisers, David and his wife make it a point that these children are helped.

To top off David's efforts, UNICEF awarded him the "Children's Champion Award" because of his extended work to uplift these communities. His passion and big heart make him a role model on and off the field, and it makes you ask yourself, "What excuse do I have not to help others?"

Chapter 6:

Legacy, Potential & Inspiration

David Ortiz is one of the rare superstars in baseball who is able to project a larger-than-life persona while still being relatable to the fans.

When David first came to the Red Sox, he was surrounded by much bigger names who were highly regarded around the league. Stars like Nomar Garciaparra, Manny Ramirez, and Pedro Martinez were the clear leaders on the team.

Even during his time with the team, David was lucky enough to welcome great players such as

Mike Lowell, Josh Beckett, Curt Schilling, and Adrian Gonzalez to the Sox. However, none of them continued with the team as long as David has, and none can call themselves three-time champions with the franchise.

There is no doubt that great Boston players such as Manny, Curt, Nomar, and Pedro are all-time great players and will all most likely go down as Hall-of-Famers. However, there is a different and unique connection that David has with the city.

Some people who are not Bostonians or Red Sox fans probably wonder how/why Boston and Papi have such a symbiotic relationship. When you really dive into it, it is not that surprising. Let's first look at the history of the Red Sox, the Boston fan base was so starved for a championship that they were desperate for any player that could come along and change their luck. The "Curse of the Bambino" was real to many a fan.

On the flip side, let's look at David's history. David knows a ton about adversity and adjusting to life's challenges. After finishing school in the Dominican Republic, David signed with the

Mariners organization in early 1992. However, he had to wait five years before getting a shot at the professional level. Even when he did, he bounced from the Mariners to the Twins and in between the majors and minors, without any manager or fan base ever really giving him their full trust. Nobody during that time thought "this is our guy".

Boston was different. He quickly gelled with the players in the clubhouse, the blue collar culture of the Boston people, and even the love/hate relationship that the Boston fans are known for. But winning leads to more love than hate, and Papi gave them what they so desperately wanted.

As far as his personality, David can be both very emotional and also rather calm, depending on the circumstance. He knows who to interact with and how to interact with them. This is the reason he can mesh with such a variety of personalities. Many players would call him "the most respected" player on the team at this point in his career.

He has also gained a few different nicknames during his time with the Sox. Other than the commonly known, "Big Papi", he also goes by

"Señor Octubre" and "Cooperstown". If this doesn't show the love that Sox fans have for him, consider the fact that he actually came in third in the voting for Boston's mayoral race in 2013.

Conclusion

I hope this book was able to help you gain inspiration from the life of David Ortiz, one of the best players currently playing in Major League Baseball.

The rise and fall of a star is often the cause for much wonder. But most stars have an expiration date. In baseball, once a star player reaches his mid- to late-thirties, it is often time to contemplate retirement. What will be left in people's minds about that fading star? In David's case, people will remember how he came onto the scene for the Red Sox and delivered for the fans. He will be remembered as the guy who helped his team build their image by winning multiple championships, while building his own image along the way.

Charismatic, laid-back, yet intimidating, this Boston Red Sox DH has baseball fans in awe with a playing prowess that sportswriters say is comparable to that of the legendary, Ted Williams.

David has also inspired so many people because he is the star who never fails to connect with fans and give back to the less fortunate. Noted for his ability to impose his will on any game, he is a joy to watch on the baseball field. Last but not least, he's remarkable for remaining simple and firm with his principles in spite of his immense popularity.

Hopefully you learned some great things about David in this book and are able to apply some of the lessons that you've learned to your own life! Good luck in your journey!

Made in the USA
San Bernardino, CA
20 March 2017